THE QUEEN OF LOST BAGGAGE

For Marjorie and Eric:

May you catch tigers in red weather, on whatever coast, in whichever season.

THE QUEEN OF LOST BAGGAGE

Barbara F. Lefcowitz

WASHINGTON WRITERS' PUBLISHING HOUSE
Washington, D.C.
1986

ACKNOWLEDGMENTS

Grateful acknowledgment is given to the following journals, where some of these poems first appeared or will soon appear:

ANTIETAM REVIEW; BOGG; KAYAK; THE LITERARY REVIEW; MINNESOTA REVIEW; MONTPELIER; PLUS FOUR; OUTERBRIDGE; OXFORD MAGAZINE; PAINTED BRIDE QUARTERLY; POET LORE; PRAIRIE SCHOONER (Reprinted by permission of University of Nebraska Press. ©1980 University of Nebraska Press); THE RECONSTRUCTIONIST; THE WASHINGTON REVIEW; THE WEBSTER REVIEW; THE WINDLESS ORCHARD.

"The Witch's Testimony" appeared as well in *The Wild Piano* (Dryad, 1981).

Also by Barbara F. Lefcowitz:

A Risk of Green (Gallimaufry Press: Washington, D.C. 1978)
The Wild Piano (Dryad Press: Washington and San Francisco, 1981)

The author wishes to express her gratitude to the National Endowment for the Arts Literature Program for a fellowship in Creative Writing and to the Rockefeller Foundation for a residency at the Bellagio Study and Conference Center in Italy, where a portion of this book was written and revised. And a special acknowledgement of gratitude to my husband, Allan, for his assistance with typesetting and consistent support of poetry in general, these poems in particular.

Typeset at The Writer's Center, Bethesda, Maryland.
Printed in the United States of America. All rights reserved.
ISBN 0-931846-29-3   LC 85-052078

Cover design, including an original etching, by Janice Olson.
Layout by Kathryn E. King.

WASHINGTON WRITERS' PUBLISHING HOUSE
PO Box 50068
Washington, D.C. 20004

First Edition
First Printing, 1986

TABLE OF CONTENTS

THE BIRTHDAY: after Chagall

Absurd to think you could survive
   so far from water
      my body's inmost colors.

But have no fear:
   the milk-glass, the melon, the blood-
      red carpet of morning

will never penetrate your dream-lids.
   From my own wide open eyes
      again you unfurl,

float to the bed where I made you up,
   your collar's tab a small wing.
      Never to be quite the same, my

acrobat-angel, green and black night-son,
   tethered to me by invisible threads.
      Hurry. You must not linger.

The flowers, too, reject this glare,
   drift towards the window,
      begin to fade like day-stars.

No one but I will believe them
   or the stretchmarks that bloom
      night after night when I bear you again.

THE FORGOTTEN

Solid as the nickel
whose glint I saw once
under an iron-meshed subway grate,
all of the world's forgotten
belongs to you,
crafty old shoplifter
who tricks the most cleverly hidden cameras,
brazenly roams through our stockrooms
stuffing whole racks of gold-smocked days
into your hefty pockets; jugs of brandied words
we thought we could live off forever.

Even the Greeks forgot to name you,
confused you with underworld rivers,
lethal flowers.
Hell, you're no more a bearer of lotus
than poor Mrs. Tuvnik, who took a scissors
to the other patients' snapshots,
and only rarely is it kindness
that makes you scald the labels
from our jars, wipe the ink from a face
before we can print its furrows,
deny exit visas
to the refugees huddled in dream-steerage.

By now you've amassed so much loot
you've forgotten
where it's buried, or why each day
you put on your coat of pockets,
set out to forget some more.

THE REMEMBERED

1. *To Memory*

Disheveled old girl, will you
ever stop flirting with the busboy, wagging
your henna curls in the Schlitz-gilded mirror?
My order slipped again
through your brain's flowerets,
you giggle, sashay from the kitchen,
slap down the same flash-frozen wafer-steaks
you've been serving for years.
No chocolates, each silver-wrapped rose
packed with surprise; no eggs
with feathery blood-threads inside,
not even the plum
I must have split open
under the porch-lace four decades back.

So you've stalked me to the flea market.
As if I didn't know your tricks,
the pins without clasps,
knobless radios,
pans of dead cake.
The remembered. Who has ever made a light
from the wickless candles
you hawk in the name of the remembered?

And now you beat the door,
beg me to take you in.
No one more lonely than memory,
all those faces and names, stories
you can never tell.
Too late.
I've replaced you with a gallery of portraits
drawn from memory.

2. *From Memory*

For him
for my monocled
charcoal-haired sleuth
I display the fingerprints,
bloodstains, hooked motives
to fasten your story.
And for you, foolish host,
some red herrings, quicksilver clues.

For him, not for you,
I dangle the rope
you once twisted to make a swing,
release the little tune
you just whistled, tease you
with the tang of Greek lemons,
bubbah's milk-sour rags.

Inside your skin
I've set up my Devonshire cottage,
my desk, my files of intricate plots,
the detective I love more than
royalties, Hollywood, prizes.

For him, not for you,
I make up your story.

MEMOIRS OF AN AMNESIAC

A woman who had suffered a nearly total loss of memory was found wandering in a park near Fort Lauderdale, Florida . . . Even after widely televised publicity led to a reunion with her family, she claimed that she was so fond of the court-assigned name Jane Doe she would keep it as her own.

—The Washington Post 4/81

i.

I'm the queen of lost baggage.
Pure jazz.
Your dream that swam off with the bait.

Down a ramp
into black water
each day's tightly roped sack
carries me off.
I've forgotten why

I can't remember who I am where I was what I'm for.

Hello, I'm Jane Doe. Has
anyone a story to spare—
a twist of hair, worn music,
a jolly old aunt?

ii.

My family of mirrors
is friendly but ceremonious.
Always I must flash a calling card.

Hello, I'm Jane Doe. Today
I'm your valentine girl, decked out
on a spray of black lace. Today
your marzipan bride. Do not try

to reclaim your silver and jewels;
my fingerprints vary like snow-crystals.

Cameras are shy. How I must embarrass
their wide stupid eyes. I'm the blur
in the back row, the jagged streak
that cuts the name from the face behind you.

iii.

My curriculum is tough but timely:
COMPARATIVE LINGUISTICS: the verb *to be* in Dance, Wind, Snake
The Shapes of Smoke.
MUSICOLOGY: The Gavotte in B flat for Roof and Rain.
GEOGRAPHY: how to get from X to Y via burned bridges,
obliterated paths, duplicities, mendacities.
HOME ECONOMICS: the art of spring cleaning when you have no
closets, jars, boxes, tins.

iv.

The truth: I cannot lie.
All of my lies are lies.
The art of lying
is intimately connected with the art of remembering.
The art of remembering
is intimately connected with the art of printmaking.
My fingerprints, you may recall, vary like snow-crystals.
Hello, I'm Jane Doe,
the super-monolinguist,
untranslatable as a pun.
My only nostalgia is for the present.

v.

When all your disguises curl up,
3 a.m. or that little crook in a conversation,
the words stumbling back to their corners
sweaty and slightly bruised, grateful
for a gulp of gatorade,
you can visit me

your ad-hoc committee of one, your star
performer, the girl that you keep in your attic
so the circus won't get her.

Hello, I'm Jane Doe.

vi.

Throw out the dried flowers, old summers
glinting in jam jars, all the keys and lockets.

I burst through the morning's egg
onto your breakfast tray.

Lost baggage.
Jazz.
The dream that swam off with the bait.

SELECTED CORRESPONDENCE OF SLEEPING BEAUTY

1. *Letter from the Palace Crones*

Dear Beauty,
Go back to bed.
Let us stitch up your sleep,
ripped at the seams like an outgrown chemise,
your skin stretching the last tatters
to scrawny lace.
Even our tarnished old eyes
will weep when you blink into the late 20th century.

This time, Beauty, there will be no kisses,
emeralds and cream, weekends in Nice.
The white-smocked princes will rise and enter
to skewer your dreams on their shiny picks.
Does Beauty still bleed, will she
sweat and shiver, endorse
this mattress, that pill? They'll tug
at your red silk tongue,
spread you open like a centerfold
to nail between
their moth-eaten beaver pelts.

2. *Beauty's Lie: To Her Biographers, Imitators,*
and Other Solipsistic Fans

I shut my eyes and music becomes bright linen
suspended from the braided wind.

Over carved flames the roast no longer crackles.
Sleep and the whole world sleeps with you.

The stone clouds will hover,
birds remain lacquered to sky
until I unlatch the velvet rope,
    flee my hall of mirrors.

Sleep and the whole world sleeps with you.
Tinted mirrors rainbow my pallor,
soft mirrors curve to a silver egg.

The stars will resume their death-watch
only when I do.

3. *Letter from Her Ugly Sisters*

Dear Beauty,

You're back on our shelf now.
   Your glaze of sleep
      gone to shavings
         bits of glitter
            on our rags and scrapers

        How we love
      to trace the cracks
    in your china-doll skull,
  pluck at your
tea-rose brain.

So you'd wake as Boadicea
   in black satin?
      Hot Ginger Brunhilde
         belting her honey-packed songs
           into the bleachers?

       No use rubbing off
    our muddy red kisses.
  Beauty, you're back on our shelf now
 with the torn wings, scraps of moon,
gutted violins.

When we twist the stem
   inside your chipped skirts
      you'll sing all night
        I am dull I am ordinary
      I'm awake and real.

4. *Beauty's Truth: To Her Princes*

All these years
you've confused me with some cataleptic princess
splayed on a raft of porcelain roses,
the palace crones whispering
menarche, the curse, the bloody curse.

Friends, lovers, pucker-lipped sycophants:
you've missed the point.
I'm the thorn in your side
that keeps you awake.
Even when you swear you've cracked my spine
I feast on your little blood-spurts,
grow fat as a cactus, shred
the quilted afternoons
you would wrap tightly around you.
Pull me out by the roots
and boredom will weigh you down
like a stillborn child, weariness
settle on your brain like a fur cap.
Staked in your rose-patch
you'll lure me back, your skins spread
for my succulent fangs,
your prickly skull my victory crown.

5. *Post-Script*

Night after night I mount you,
rub my ripe garlic clove,
my pungent grasses,
against your sprawled flanks,
singing,
always singing,
Beauty shall sleep no more.

THE SECRET OLYMPICS

In the secret olympics the gymnast unfurls
above the bars and balance-beam,
her body a luminous shawl.

Another leaps backward, leaps
until she lands in her grandmother's
wheat field. It is the 19th century, ripe

sheaves fan from her hands,
the only applause
a clatter of ladles and milk-cans.

In the secret olympics the diver
plunges forever through layers of blue,
his body's shell greeted by cheers,

towels, embraces. The marathon
runner turns right
into his middle-age, up a narrow path

through the long black tunnel, eyes
shut, feet burled and stiff; running,
still running, he glides

into the colliseum where faces
random as the yet unborn
toss elegiac roses.

In the secret olympics we discard
our thick bodies like winter coats,
wave to ourselves from pinwheeling stars.

WHY I'VE BECOME A YANKEE FAN

Where are you now, Al Gionfriddo? And you, Sydelle
Starlight, nee Sadie Lichtenstern, now that The War is over. How
you loved to click your heels in the bricked-in courtyards, henna
ringlets crowning your Air Raid Warden uniform, your voice so
powerful it could extinguish all the lights in Brooklyn. It is
for you that in this, my first bi-focular autumn, I have become a
Yankee fan.

There were rumors, Sydelle, that the little crease of a widow
who lived in apartment 4B was so shaken by your vibrato she
snuffed out the *yahrzeit* candle she had lit for the anniversary
of her husband's death. And in this, my first bi-focular autumn,
there are rumors that the entire country is going blonde. Blonde
astroturf lawns are spreading over the suburbs, the cornfields,
the backroads, the inmost clefts of the inner city. Even the
weeds are blonde: the new office buildings wear blonde wigs and
wink their fresh blue eyes. Albert Francis Gionfriddo, 5'6", 165
pounds, who on 5 October 1947 in the 6th inning of World Series
game 6 between the Yankees and the Dodgers leaped so high into
the rich silvery sky above Yankee Stadium that you floated over
the boroughs into my Brooklyn bedroom—where are you now,
Al Gionfriddo?

From *The Collected Essays* of Carl Furillo: "In the blurry
margin between distance and reading vision, all objects assume
their shadows or reveal a hitherto unsuspected identical twin."
Last week, in the blonde, scrubbed suburb where I live out my
autumns, a neighbor—decent, efficient, Unitarian, a devotee of
granola bagels—slipped a *yahrzeit* candle into the sterno ring
under her chafing dish. I was amused. But surely, you say, one
such desecration is not sufficient cause to become a Yankee fan?

Ah, but there were other lights in Brooklyn, lights even your
voice could not put out. Like the lights shining all night in
the offices above Ebbets Field, cigar-chomping men rubbing their
palms over colossal mounds of cash—no matter that the Yankees,

19

MYOPIA

We lived in our own soft country,
lightbulbs hazed to snow-moons,
the sleek arms of chairs
puffed with fur.
Some things completely dissolved;
scowls, knobs, the boundaries
between father and mother.
Swarms of grain, long silver threads,
where the mirror used to shine.

Until they caught us, force-
fed us carrot juice, made
our eyes ache with muscle knots
and slung across them two round lenses,
so we would see it all *their* way:
    The stars small sharp tacks.
    Beads of discrete rain.
    Each voice, each color,
    bound and hard.

Little do they know
we are only *gastarbeiter*
re-entering, always re-entering,
our own soft country
just beyond the two ground lenses,
where no one can prove
an orange wedge is not a slice of fire.

THE MUSIC

Alacazam. The tapedeck obliges,
a quicksilver purl of a waltz, Galway on flute.

Elegantly, oh so elegantly,
the starlings respond. With the newly torn leaves
and blown trash they whirl and glide

and it's better than some long ago NY Dee-Jay's
"Make Believe Ballroom Time." Sashes

of billowing silt. Graciously the dump truck
joins the cotillion of passing cars,
traffic lights politely nod from their yellow bonnets

and I marvel
how it all depends on the music, my music—

A 1928 rendition of *West End Blues*.
Birds, leaves, bits of glass
recede, take their places like fresh stars;

a single brass wave, wind merged
with my own body, the passing cars,

and I am sure
how it all depends on the music, my music—

So what can I say when a tattooed pickup
cuts in from nowhere, swaggers,
rips the soft folds of a Mozart concertina—

Shriek of brakes. Random birdcries,
leaf-packs on stampede
in the brawling wind.

What can I say
but that nothing depends on the music,
my music—

Or what can I say
when the whole car is crackling
with Jelly Roll Morton's *Red Hot Pepper Stomp*
and nothing outside so much as flickers

MEDITATIONS FROM A TRAIN WINDOW

1. *The Amtrak Mattresses*

Behold the great flotilla of mattresses.
Plump mattresses with blonde curls,
withered candy-stripers, buttonless
queens with black-eyed susans, furze-
covered skin.
        All sprawled
on the Amtrak roadbed, flung
from Hopper-green windows,
    bungalows scrawled
on Jersey rust farms, hungover
hospitals.

   Is it a curse:
From Baltimore to Newark You Shall Sleep No More
or a citizens' revolt against old sweat
sag and grime?

   Birds
pluck away at the mattress guts. Hair,
crusts of sleep
   scattered to the rusting wheat.

2. *The Amtrak Bathtub*

It would have been the perfect bath.
Steamier than the swoon
of deep maroon water
at Mrs. Doolan's B & B in County Clare,
steeped with more sulfur than Carracalla.
Odalisque of the rails,
more bouyant than Archimedes,
I would have floated clear
to Hoboken Harbor, but the tub,
its flanks tinged with festering rainbows,
was in a field south of Philly
and it was miles before the towel appeared,

nubs and fringe on a snag of fence,
further still
the plug, faucet, creme de menthe suds.
By the time the woman ran along the tracks,
peeling off clothes
until her inmost rags and lace,
I had long ago left the train.

3. *Riding the Amtrak Way*

If a wild bedspring broke from its root
& pistons rushed from a tangled
boxcar with great blooms
of rust; if the fangs

of an umbrella-carcass pierced the last
living mattress & a kelly-
green mannequin soared through pondcrust
on a washtub, Botticelli

would set up his easel near Baltimore,
bring forth a maiden, her shell
delicate as April. Even Hieronymous Bosch
would ignore Sweet Buckle Creek's gush

of gaudy polyester fish, paisley
& festered plaid. A sky more Flemish
than Jersey, here a winged herring, there
a lusty peasant swilling beer
from a cracked eggshell. Cheers!

Make way for Monet. A shirtsleeve
dangling from Paradise Mills
floats onto his lily pad.

When Fra Angelico dreams in Worcester
of a pink small hand
sprouting through the rot & reliquary trash
he remembers only chariots, a golden band
riding towards Tuscany.

TRAFFIC LIGHTS

Bless the traffic lights,
triple-eyed tamers of steel beasts,

who nod from their bonnets
like pious farmwives,
who sway in the wind to our deepest music;

more faithful than the moon
their ritual blink and shine.

When they redden, giant roses
with taut petals, the endings
of all our nerve-flowers
comply at once, old lusts
we would consummate if we dared,
the long sheer promise of starlit freeways.

We rehearse our endless scenario
of endings; curtains, kaput, farewell,
the little pause between beats
that one day will sustain its final note,
our hearts stunned to stone.

More green than summer islands
their emerald stare
shocks our clocks alive again.
We run through fresh grass and
long dead parents beam their smiles:
Go, go, we will always be here
to applaud your somersaults, your
slide through the sea's rim.

When their eyes coat yellow
our oldest warning signs flash:
change, danger, falling rocks, unhealed scars,
this road goes nowhere
but its own ending.

Bless the traffic lights,
mute witnesses to our incessant errands.
At night when their pallettes are dimmed
to feeble blinks, they gossip in secret,
click up the day's toll.
No matter how many happy journeys—
the flower-strewn wedding car,
the convertible loaded with prom dancers,
the coupe whose black shell
seals our deepest music,
gently they nod across empty corners,
life goes on,
death goes on.

THE RED EYE FROM OAKLAND TO NEWARK

"The captain is drunk
and has temporarily misplaced the aircraft."

On channel three of my stereo headset
Itzhak Perlman was playing *Chocolate Apricots*.

When he asked us to refrain
from stomping on the clouds
my legs became fragile as a heron's.

"Please remember: smoking is permitted
only from crests and plumes, most birds
have limited luggage capacities.

If you are lucky enough to find an egg
breathe normally.
Those of you travelling with small children
should take them home at once."

From Itzhak's violin two Schubert chords
escaped to the exit doors, we slid
down their silvery purls
into the roar and sheer blue.

"The captain has been taken into custody
by radar control."
Beaming from Nightline's three cameras
he assures Ted Koppel
the plane has been found:
slipped through a seam in Nevada's hip pocket,
hitching a ride from the wind,
munching the border between Missouri and Kansas.

Breathe normally.

"Four people can marry
but only two can have a child,"
the man across the aisle whispered,
his beak gently piercing
my deepest wish, deepest fear, nothing
to snag the loops of giddy soar and dip.

It was then that I waved to myself.
More bored than amazed, she waved back,
clinked the ice in her cup,
studied the ribbons of weather
in yesterday's *USA Today*.

"Remember," the stewardess crooned
through a yellow megaphone, "keep
your airbelts loosely fastened."

"Each of us began—no exceptions—
with someone else's ecstasy."

BALKAN ROSES

1. *On the Road to Sarajevo*

Pinch the earth, this is Bosnia-Herzegovina.
The olive trees the gnarled
old women with bundles of gorse on their backs

don't give a damn this is Bosnia-Herzegovina.
In the mauve stucco room, Tito
framed with seashells

above a scorched madonna,
I dream about travelling to Bosnia-Herzegovina.
Nikonije savresen . . . Nobody's perfect,

they greet us in Anglo-Croatian
at the Labyrinth Bar in Mostar.
Bruno from the Turist Biro

unwraps a poison piano, one
certain chain of random chords
and you're gone. By the tenth glass of wine

it is next winter. I dream about dreaming
of travelling to Bosnia-Herzegovina, wine-
glass in hand, the old loneliness tango.

On an island called Hvar
the lavendar swayed like surf
but the stones were too steep:

to get there pinch the earth.
A peasant sells home-bottled wine, roses
rush from her teeth into a village wedding.

Pinch the earth, this is Bosnia-Herzegovina.
Soon we will reach Sarajevo, 1914,
the nightmares.

2. *The Widows of Sibenik: for Mica and Rosa*

I sing for the widows of Sibenik
  bring them red flowers
in the crypt by the old walls of Sibenik
    wooden table chipped bench
  where they'll sit
     seven years

    black stockings black
      sweaters black smocks
   the little wells behind their eyes
 dry as the 13th century cistern
that once held the waters of Sibenik
    An American bomb cracked its heart

    And all the black dye in Dalmatia
would not be enough for their penitence
   Only the dead can hide deeper
 than the widows of Sibenik
   Only the dead can bring flowers
    to the widows of Sibenik

    The bouquet I presented
  now paper and string
I fumble my abundant hair
   to small black knots
     our only lingua franca
   for years I'll hear them
    breathing black
   old sisters
  younger than I
    where did you hide my red flowers

3. *On the Ferry, Eastbound, from Hvar to Split*

Dovidjenja! The tough
dark men
wave roses, beer, goodbye
to the village
the stone-domed church
kerchiefed mothers waving roses
A seam of lights
we separate to Split
the village
a thin white spine
an eyelid a blink
Nobody travels alone
The old men play cards
a Croatian from Australia
brags about his gripes
the robust wine
His accent ropes us in
closer than we care
Even the islands
melt and link arms
a Partisan song
"Country Roads" with
melancholy Slavic twang
Tell me this isn't
almost heaven
the Shenandoah River has not
entered the Adriatic
Each of us will not
collect his secret cargo
on the gangplank to Split
A seam of lights
torn by tough dark men
kerchiefed mothers waving roses
to the westbound loaded ferry

CIRCA BERKELEY

I. TELEGRAPH AVENUE
—For the Bubble Lady

Rag-robed mendicant,
your baked smile doesn't fool me.
There you go again,
waving your wand at whoever passes,
the blue al fresco church festooned
with your soap and water blessings.
So what's your price today, lady?
My string-bag of old country nostrums,
my books, Stolichnaya, heretic charms?
In Assisi I met you disguised,
a crippled nun. *Buon giorno, benedizione!*
After the last tour bus
you swirled up the crooked streets
swinging your crutches. At Kennedy Airport
you pinned me with chrysanthemum.
Old Granny Elixir, you swapped roots for coins,
gaunt in your torn babushka at the market in Zagreb.

How could I let you come so close? Can't you see
I'm invisible?
Fresh bubbles splash my hair and eyes,
balloon my skull with marble sheen.
You smile.
And dammit, I'm smiling too,
all the way to the Campanile,
smiling wide as a gondola,
the great icon bridge to my west.
O Lady of Simple Blessings, go.
Pipe your pastel madness on.

—For the Stowaway

Familiar stranger
hook-toothed crone
what lazy border guard
let you enter my rented California?

34

Always you wait for the sun.
A brood of blue eyes
blinks through the fog. I
flip on my mask, comic, awry,
wave to the goats, the spastic clown,
the ragdoll flopped by The Dirty Rainbow,
the tin-cup cellist and bedroll trumpeteer,
wave until you tug me
through the day's gold rim,
sling your rope around me, swing
me all the way east
to the dark foyer
I thought I had long ago fled.

When I leave this unmet summer
you'll greet me oh yes
you'll greet me at my door
with lush whispers:
run out and play
it's sinful to hide from the sun.

II. OBJECT FOUND AT THE BERKELEY MARINA:
—*For the Indian, the Strangers, and the Tin-cup Cellist*

Far from the sea
that delivers it whole
a ring of jelly-sheathed towers
joined by gut and string,
bloody eggs in a bramble nest
rock-rooted so hard
no matter how I pull
nothing loosens.
The two crackless shells:
if I pry them to a grin
surely the pungent secret
will be mine—
whatever collusion of bone and slime
makes this wholeness,
whatever liason of
beach, rock, feet, eye and hand

makes me break
village from beach-root,
prop it by ashtray and bedside clock.

Tonight no one stops
for the tin-cup cellist.
Outside my window
the Indian breathes
into his solitary shank-flute.
Strangers float by. Joined, unjoined,
I listen to chipped voices,
driftwood hands and feet,
our crack-shelled fears
scattering toward separate seas.

III. FOR THE GOLDEN GATE BRIDGE (upon walking across)

Red harp, plane
that wobbles on take-off,
your lanes sway
on the brain's calamity-map. And why
am I doing this? No suspension
from fear, sky
over chain-slung bay: which way
home? Return would be as crazy.
Grandma Annie cranes from the rails,
crosses from Brooklyn to the Triangle Shirt Factory,
ca. 1904. Red bicycles, red bones, plain
concrete, the feet, the feat: to chord
the floating city with your
steel red strings.

I'll walk you better with my eyes
when I dream a return to the distant marina,
to the bar disguised as a ship,
where once the Bay rolled me eastward,
rolled me inward and backward—
You, the great icon bridge,
more aloof with each sip
until I was home, the villagers
eager for jewels from my emigrant lips.
How the city, white queen,
was guarded by four golden ropes.
How her slopes gleamed with coins.
Better any place than where we are,
where we've actually been.
Red harp restrung from mid-air.

SEA-LINK

—for Allan

Ireland made us young.
The bed and breakfast mothers,
soft and bumpy as scones,
serving jugs of warm milk,
hot-water bottles for the rain-thatched bed.
Doreen Burke, who told us
the Burren bloomed at night with fairies.
We listened without a wink or snicker.
Mr. O'Connail, retired Dublin cop,
come west to keen and curse the century,
"All you young folks either lazy or crazy,"
in Europe's last house
high on Slea Head across from the Great Blasket Island
which has been hitching a ride to America
so many years now it might as well
rock in the sea, feed a few sheep, read
all about itself in the National Geographic.

And Ireland made us older than we dare admit.
The student from Galway, fire-cracker eyes,
who dared us to define
democracy, America, free will, the good life,
before we could skim the cream from our Guinness.
Foolish questions, we shrugged:
You who can name ships, flowers, battles, cows,
the GNP of every western country,
I who would rather dance than know the steps.
On Sea-Link from Dun Laoghaire to Holyhead
we ferry east to fly west.

SUNDAY NIGHT AT THE GYLDENLOVE HOTEL, OSLO

Oh, go take a picture, get laid
by a Danish sailor, anything
but another tourist poem,
its snapshot insights
packed with such privileged urgency
surely the suitcase will burst,
fling words all over Karl Johan Street,
where a woman with a woodcut face
will pick one up, walk right back
into Munch's "Anxiety." The old man
I left at the bar will pick up
another word, sorry it's so cold, so dry—
but surely a poem is better
than a one-night stand; it's a
lifetime sentence, a pure monogamous marriage.
Where else put on such thickly knit robes
as "the exuberance of Munch's melancholia"
or "the peculiar solace of a foreign silence?"
Now the lobby's empty, nothing but a
blond TV Elvis, "Are You Lonesome Tonight?"
in Anglo-Norsk. What the hell, we poets
all are tourists, in our own houses,
even there, we're always lugging and packing,
looking for that one secret door
down the stairless dark
that will make us the genuine traveller.

GREEN ROCK

In the harbor, shining
emerald slab, red and plum whorls
interlaced, the grooved frequencies
of ancient trade routes.
I would come back with notepad and winejug,
my claim staked with a braid of kelp,
measured steps.

How can I know now
if it's slipped back to sea
or perhaps never been there at all,
like the young balladeer,
her voice whorled with sadness
old as fishwives and spicewives,
I once heard, thought I heard,
halfway down Shop Street in Galway.

POKEBERRIES

Gypsy-colored trinkets packed
with poison, they arrive
with October's demands
for danger and sleep,
dangle between the splintery branches.
Pick. Crush. Lick the stain.

Nothing happens.

At the National Cancer Institute
three blocks north,
flirtations far less frivolous.
Or so we would believe
the earnest proud physicians
assaulting manic villages.
Extracts from deadly bark.
Bright berries hauled in by the latest caravan.

Better the well-rehearsed story.
Quilts, frayed melodies
that briefly return
the distant children
from their gypsy disguises.
As if anything could hold
such recollection.
What berries remain
I collect with gloved hands,
dump into jars.

As if I didn't know
that in a few days, like ripe green stones
scooped from the beach, they'll have lost
all their brilliance. A stench
so unbearable I'll toss them to the squirrels,
who perhaps will be cured to wolves,
perhaps to death.

The physicians write
their inconclusive reports:
neither hope nor despair.
Already one-eyed winter
prepares its potions. Monochrome.
Neither deadly nor healing.

CONDOM FOUND OFF CRESCENT HARBOUR

I cannot swear
it's not some rare northern sea-bloom,
fucus vesicolus, spermathamnion tuneri,
faintly green-rashed mauve
like a rose-mallow tongue,
perfectly parabolic with a dab
of tickler-moss
dangling from its grape-shaped sac.
When I dredged it up from the tidal pool,
its gelatinous sheen stuck to my fingers
and the thing nearly shredded.
Tiny clouds of worms puffed in my palm.
I licked them and they tasted like ancient Viking,
o what layers of toil and heave, how many tides
and gnashing storms, deep green swoons of surf
had pelted my sea-worn surprise?
How many dark folded inlets were breached,
euthora cristata, prophyra umbilacalus,
and left keening?
Yes, an old mosser confirms, it's the real thing,
prized for its succulent essence—
cramps, wounds, catarrh—there's nothing
it won't cure.

METAMORPHOSIS

Today I will change the world
by learning five new words in demotic Greek.

Bread, I transform you to *psomi,*
so close to *soma,* the body.
Wonder-bread, spice-grained, black-veined,
I take you in.

Appletree outside my window,
you become *milea,* red clusters
glow now from your snow-crusted branches.

If only I can keep the words
from escaping to their native country—

Renamed *loulouthia*, flowers on my bathrobe
sway loose, ring the moon, *fengarri*,
a finger tipped with Adriatic light.

If only I can keep the words—

tattered and scarred from their stubborn resistance,
the newly caught words
that refuse my thin soup; buck and shy
as I slip on the handcuffs,
coop them in cells already packed
with truculent syllables,

sentence them for life.

THE DECLINE OF LANGUAGE

Next Tuesday (a lean slippery *face*)
you'll be starting school (a silvery *lozenge*)
my father told me as we walked down the street.
A teacher (very tall, her *purple satin* gown
            pools at her feet)
will make you learn
    that Tuesday follows Monday
    schools are for alphabets
    teachers are called Miss Dayton
    and smell from Vicks

Many years later
on an island in Casco Bay
I saw Wednesday again:
a swatch of rough brown *carpet*.
And remembered June:
reddish, swollen, like a giant *tangerine* lobe.
Friday is a crispy *wheel*.

I wish I could recall
what a face looks like;
a lozenge, purple satin, tangerine, wheel.

RUMPELSTILTSKIN'S REVENGE

Stacks, loaves,
honeypots of warm gold.
Your hands and hair
sticky with loot, even then
you suspected
that naming me once
would not do, swaddled the child
with leftover sheaves, swore
satisfaction with things as they were.

I hid, healed, changed my name,
hissed you to a tryst
under the appletrees. After that
it was easy. I was your genie,
your stockbroker, hotline,
fix-it man, muse-in-the-box,
your demands more absurd
with each moulting.
How to spin fog to fresh wool;
snip the flight of a bird;
weave shaggy sleep into rugs.

My price never changed.
Caspar, Melchior, Balthazar, Sheepshanks!
You jiggled your alphabet dice,
named me
and nabbed me.
Heh, heh, lovely princess,
have I got a trick.
Any day now I'll bang
at the palace's gate,
a maundering beggar,
utterly nameless.

Wolfrit! you'll cry. Silberchtus! Adolald!
I'll shake my head, fill my sacks
with your brats. No matter
how hard you try you won't
get them back. I'll set them to work
whittling names
from the trees, blacking out street signs,
unchristening faces
as if they were jars with torn labels.
Say hello to yourself,
spinster princess,
the name of the game.

WHY ESKIMOS LOVE ICE CREAM AND GOD IS AN ATHEIST

No, you've got it all wrong.
It was the ancient zero
that never took the Greeks
into its calculations,
like the modern melody
has cut its ties to music,
fled to where the blues are so sky
no one dares sing them.

    Is that why the Eskimos
    have 46 varieties of snow
    for words?
    How do they keep their lips
    from freezing, their books from melting?

The same way your cake bakes the oven.

    How simplistic. Now you'll say
    that the Navajos have no time for words.

Actually I was thinking about Finland.
The Finns, my dear, have no future.

    That makes me uneasy. Like when I saw
    his dog walking my dentist.

And what if he was?
Could not the dog have perceived
from a certain rhythm of scratching and pacing,
a fecund restiveness as it were,
that it was time to walk your dentist?

    You're losing me completely now,
    like my umbrella last week
    left me in some dark vestibule.

So literal. No wonder you always prefer the missionary position.

But I disagree with nearly all
of the missionary positions—
on the cultural depravity of the Indians,
the monolithic godhead—

Good. We've come full circle,
put the cart back behind the horse
where it has always belonged.

Ah, so it was the wheel after all,
that remained ignorant of the Incas—
probably for excellent reasons—
the neutron bomb that kept itself aloof
from all centuries preceding this one—
again, one must suppose, for excellent reasons—
Beethoven's music
that hid silently in the wings
waiting for Beethoven to be born.

MY POETRY RETIREMENT DINNER

Who will attend:

All my dark wild love-children.
The brash early hits I can barely recall.
Crew-cut epigrams.

O bashful unnoticed ones chainsmoking out by the potted palms:
My apologies.

Anorexic haiku nibble the celery . . .   The sweat-suited breath-
less enjambements! The sonnets still doing yoga
to stretch their spines, the stuttering consonances, clip-nailed
end-rhymes, caesuras, shoplifted imports!

Hello there, well-published wunderkinder. You look so lovely
at the dias; your gold braid and designer smiles.
Don't stare at the stunted ones, drooling and sucking their thumbs,
the thigh-slapping garlic-breathed failures,
beer-bellied villanelles telling their same yellowed jokes
over and over and over.

Ah, here come the ones I never wanted.
And yes,
   the few miracles.

How they will get there:

On the Hoboken Ferry, the Culver Line, the shadows of leaves.
Some will fly all night on the red-eye, others float up
from the ocean floor, their skins a dusky velvet;
rise from steerage still shaking the snow from their boots,
slide down a crooked bannister.

What they will do:

Shuffle their feet.
Tickle each other awake.
Diddle with their name-tags, doodle on their napkins.

Who else will attend:

My faithful readers.

Why the many empty chairs:
. . . .

The toasts:

will be offered by Miss Velma Withee, late of P.S. 179, third
period Special Progress English: "Poetry, my dear, is the
rhythmic creation of beauty" (E.A. Poe) and by Mr. Gary Blutz,
late of *The American Poultry Review, The Snortin' Anthology,
Poetry Wan, Ants Ate Us*, and numerous other publications, grateful
acknowledgement is given thereto: "Poetry Is Frozen Poetry."

A talking telegram from my fellow poets:

> Regret we cannot be with you
> On this your special day
> But we've sent some brand new verses
> (Strictly first drafts)
> Do you have something useful to say?

The gifts:

A way of happening.
A mouth.
A red red rose.
A real toad.
A blue guitar.
Thirteen blackbirds in a tamarind tree.
A mute fruit.
A sudden blow.
A frosted apple.
A multifoliate rose.

51

A bleeding swan.
A dare-gale skylark.
Thirteen blackbirds in an axle tree.
A bird that never wert.
A darkling plain.
A condominium in Innisfree.
A gold watch that ticks a heaven around the stars.
A fishing rod with invisible worms.
Thirteen blackbirds in a shoe tree.
A sick rose.
A rough beast.
Tender buttons.

What I will do afterwards:

Call my poems long distance on their birthdays.
Pack away their little cups and spoons,
their ingratitude.
Laugh like Sarah when she first felt the news.

MENOPAUSAL BASEBALL

Pre-Christmas morning born roaring
with thumbs in its ears. Please.
Someone lob my too-tautly-stitched
hungover skull
into deep green centerfield
so I need hear no more
last summer mashed, ground
by the county leaf-gatherers.

Surely no fans could make such brutal music.
They have all left with their
sunburned dreams, their hampers, kazoos,
and only I know the season's still on,
so many scoreless extra innings
I've long since lost count
when I passed nine
and how many children are never to be born.

What shells these eggs must have!
Pinks and electric greens; polka-dot, plaid,
hexagonal, trifid, polyconic, lashed
eggs that blink like eyes,
big and blue as runway lights, goose-eggs, gaudy
Ukrainian Easter eggs, *oeufs en croustades,* eggs Benedict—
All wired with mad tangles of DNA . . .

Ah, my eccentric ones. My triple-handed pianist; my
supersonic ski-jumper who never lands;
Dame Babel, a tongue for each tongue in the world.
Crazy Aunt Stella, dead from electro-shock at Creedmore
State Hospital, I present your great-grand niece. My
Pegasus; my harlequin chess king; my
wish upon a star in 38 flavors; my
let us cater your next affair; my Coronado; my Puck—

To think I've had you all my life
inside me, goodbye now and good luck,
before the game is called
because of darkness,
sweet reason, bloody riots.

GOTHEL'S LAMENT

Her hair. I'll never get rid of her hair.
It's smothered the rampion,
so many snags my sharpest rakes
snap their fangs. Her hair,
it's taken root in my rock-walled heart,
shoots through my fingertips.

The girl, sweet Rapunzel. I alone
would have the girl, the secret
lodged always inside me.

How was I to know she'd want more
than my simple food,
leave me
with only her hair, so much hair,
it's wound itself around trees,
buried whole villages; the earth's skull
will swarm with tangled blonde curls
if I don't get rid of her hair.

The more I try to slash and burn,
the tougher its strands, an epidemic,
it spreads from my hands, invades
like a celtic horde,
plumes waiving from wild plaits.

And all because
I wanted a little love
before tending my evening garden.

GRETEL'S STORY

". . . are we now out of monsters? Are we now reduced to sensible conclusion like empty water with no one more interesting than ourselves to fear?"

—*Richard Hugo, "Sneosdal"*

1. *Gretel Dreams in Middle Age*

The crusts of that old cottage
cordoned by barbed-wire brush.
And then it ends.

If she could
dream her way back, if
she could hack her way through.

Gretel
plump and fifty
dreams of geese and money.

Or a wolf disguised as Hansel
escorts her to Bonn
just as she reaches the woods.

Once at full moon
an old man strews pebbles
but their dazzle blinds her

to a patch of cabbage roses.
She takes apart their velvet eyelids
and wakes up.

If she could dream her way back,
if she could hack her way through,
the witch would be a piece of cake.

Gretel would nibble discreetly,
disarm her with sweet talk,
revamp the cottage with crisp loaves

from her own secret ovens.
Like squirrels the village children
would flock to her gingery door,

dance through the woods with her,
pluck wild apples from her apron,
pokeberries from her tangled hair.

If she could dream her way back,
if she could peel the rind
from that fragrant old story, open

its secret eye.
But Gretel the good
gingham hausfrau

shakes the crumbs from her pillow
and dreams of geese and money,
the distant children.

2. *The Return*

Oven still crackling. A twist
of her own hair on crisp linen.
Come out you wily bitch, I've made it

through the forest's black heart.
One platter. A pointed shoe with red-hot gravy
and the dark oven still crackling.

Gretel skims the kettle, rich
with old broth. Shakes out the brooms
bristle by bristle. Come out
you wily bitch, we're far
from through.

If you're hiding in a log
I'll scrape off your burls.
If you're hiding in the salad
I'll crunch you and douse you with oil.
Scare me to my roots, old shrew.

It's Gretel come back to the woods,
liebe Gretel who fetched the water for you
in those same shiny pails. Windows intact
and the oven still crackling.
No witch-bone,
no ash.

The moon, a fresh gouda,
dangles from a string. Gretel
grabs a paring knife.
No witch-bone, no ash.
Her morning face
dull as lard.

3. *The Letters to Hansel*

Dear Hansel, ex-brother, you are back
in the forest. A crust of sleep
your camouflage. My swiss army knife
scrapes off some glaze, snips
a feather from that old white bird
rippling your eyelids.
A slash clean through the crust—
I am watching the two of us
snagged in familiar bramble.
Almost I clear us through. You
hang back, something about a shiny rock.

The witch caws her hex
up the craggy slopes
of your snoring. With a
single deft motion I lop off her tongue,
skewer it on your dreampike.

Nothing wakes you up.
I pluck a berry for a souvenir.

Salmon float from their platters
onto slender forks. The host
tips his hat to reveal the Bulgarian charge d'affaires.

We speak of weighty matters, smoke Gauloises,
until the ceremony starts.

The bride carries nightshade, a sprig
of sumac. You lift her veil,
catch silver kisses in your smile.

This time there will be no rescue.
Waiters glide past, a roast
spreads its keyboard ribs.

And then the dance.
I rush through the guests crying Hansel, my Hansel—

Pardon madame? Enchante. You brush me aside
with diplomatic grace, resume
your black tango.

You are the *oberfuhrer* of shopping malls,
health spas and theme parks.

My gold-plated double, a technological wonder,
performs the oven trick with perfect timing.

Surprise! I arrive in my Gretel rags,
sell crumbs from the one and only true cottage

to the unsuspecting tourists.
You put me to work as your loss leader.

I am your own private forest.
You enter jaunty as the future,
shake your crystal balls
and spread a picnic on my
mossy clearing. Our father slogs in
from the 19th century, hones his ax,
builds a cottage with remarkable agility.
His wife lugs in the kettles,
complains she's still hungry.

And why don't you answer, dear Hansel, ex-brother?
You've nothing to say? I've wrenched all your wisdom teeth
before they could turn into pearls?
If we were hands, I'd sue you: left vs. right
for assault with the deadly weapon of indifference.
No use trying to break the mirror.
I'll show up when least expected.
In your soup.
In your beautiful suitcases.
In that little crook of the evening
where tomorrow wags its finger.

4. *The Witch's Testimony* (Epilogue)

The cat's out of the bag, my friends: I never did
get roasted in the oven. The children
concocted the whole story. Even now
I shape my bread, moist and gingery, into
cuckoo-clock houses with marzipan windowsills.

Come and take a lick. But for godssake
don't confuse me
with those crumpled women in the valium ads
or your menopausal aunts, pungent
with lemon soap and whiskey.

Of course I never meant the children
any harm. Come try my hot loaves.
I fortify them now with granola, roasted
dandelion root. And my shelves are brimming
with red jars. Never mind the nasty rumors.
Lick my platters clean. Lick the shiny pans,
my skin, my glittering eyes. Children,
come out of the woods; my house is bare now
and not a single tongue nibbles my breadstick bones.

I've heard it said
that women who concoct their houses
from marzipan and gingerbread
should never complain
when the children chip away their sticky hearts.

So of course I've no regrets.
Come and see for yourself.
This oven is big enough for all of us.

ROSIE'S BANQUET:

—for Rose Lefcowitz, 1907-1984

No kitchen more pungent
than Rosie's green hospital tent,
the nurses with floury aprons,
braids of garlic in their hair.
Through her filigree of tubes and masks
Rosie kneaded and strained, arranged
her last, most lavish, feast.

Sherry to baste the roast,
mandarin orange for the wild rice!
Her finest china
slipped from its quilted sheathe,
she laid each plate just so
on the rubbery sheet.
Mince the ginger, rinse the shallots!
Slowly, the cake must rise slowly,
each layer delicate as a moon,
o doctor, keep the oven warm,
poke your needles gently in my fragile crust.

Closing in, death dressed in his best
summer guest attire and closing
relentlessly in,
all week Rosie kept arranging
under gauze and glazed hospital eyes
the meal we would no more eat
than Brueghel's wedding feast
or that other, more solemn,
last supper.

RAIN

—for Roberto Celli

Rain sharpens the memory
and the capacity to believe,
rain and fog so opaque
they conceal everything edged,
definable, nameable.
I look out from the balcony
and must rely on what I saw
in yesterday's clear light,
must rely on faith
at once having seen
people walk the esplanade,
the contours of mountains and lake,
the green tapered flames of cypress trees.

To think the rain might also be
the patron of the imagination!
How at this moment could I
or anyone disprove
that behind that wet thick curtain
a gleaming set—
streets, jewel-stone houses from a
century yet unborn—
waits to be revealed?

Someone else, made just like me,
sings in the voice I'll never be able to master.
Perhaps I am there already,
a rain-gray memory,
a rusty icon,
while the yet unborn celebrate
their unnameable fiesta.

ALPENTRAUMER

A Cycle of Poems Written at the Villa Serbelloni, Bellagio, Italy
According to folklore, *Alpentraumer*—Alpine dreams—
are supposedly unique to this particular area of the world.

1. *To Open*

I hang the travel clothes on gilded hooks,
lock away the charms, the maps, the tickets,
my official permission to enter
the world's most elegant mind spa,

and at last I've figured how
to keep the faucet open, *aperto*,
sempre aperto, how to open
the gates, the window so wide
if there's a gust the giant cypress,
pre-historic rabbi, would sway
right inside my bidet

and I know how to open the doors—
laundry room, ironing room, WC,
numberless *salottini* for the care
and gentle cleansing of the brain.

Now I need only find
the Alpentraumer Man,
who will at my call
bear a platter of dazzling dreams, white
and magically healing, a specialty of the region,
as a friend explained—sometimes
terrifying, fingers clinging to a fringe of snow,
ropeless air; sometimes soothing as convalescence.

I try the bell above my bed.
Presto! A gold buttoned *cameriere* appears
with a bottle of *acqua minerale* and bowl of fruit.

2. *The Lid*

4:30, my second afternoon at Bellagio.
Above the fever-glazed
skin of the lake, I have
dreamt so far
only of the children,
small and restless again.
I am singing them
a nonsense verse—
two old mountain women
wear black shawls
and roll bandages from snow.

3. *Albino*

This is the opulent ship
that goes nowhere,
the ritual ship
with no rules, the ship so ancient
rumors have it
by the time Pliny boarded
its earliest secrets were rubbed away.
In the Ironing Room
the wife of an eminent scholar
warns me the controls are erratic—
yesterday she scorched a black rash
on her husband's best white shirt
though managed to erase all the creases, thank god.
No dreams without memory.
Yet with each familiar form,
no matter how vaguely creased,
I turn up the controls and press, press, press.

Perhaps my friend meant *Schwarzentraumer*.
I should be in the Black Forest
and not this villa rung by Alps
in starched white jackets. ALB: a full-length
white vestment (ML ALBA fem. ALBUS, white);
ALBINO; ALBANIA; ALBUM (L. white tablet);

ALBATROSS (2a. something that causes
persistent concern,
2b. something that makes
accomplishment particularly difficult.)

4. *Amnesia*

There are rumors the ghost of Mussolini
haunts these villages, everywhere
suspicions and signs—a profile in rock,
clues about the gold
no one has ever seen or remembers seeing,
and JFK once slept in room 12
with an unidentified blonde
whose face was cropped from the guestbook.
The two white tablets
I took last night to help me sleep
must have swelled inside
to blind white eyes, white screens
in a blacked-out theatre,
so I walk the trails to look
for what I might have dreamt,
a white flower whose name I forget and whose
petals turn gray on my fingers,
a glimpse of lake-shine,
tatters of melting snow on the mountains.
A group of German tourists ja-ja's
about the gardens, the statues, the fountains.
One of them wears white sunglasses,
the lenses themselves coated white.
I wonder if she sees white noise,
a rush of sound so insistent
and insignificant
the few real melodies become rumors.

5. Report

The impeccably casual doctor,
here for a conference on Third World Disease,
tells me over buttered breakfast rolls,
"When I ran this morning up the hill,
I thought about your *Alpentraumer*,
the strange connection, if any,
between the words *trauma* (Gk. wound) and *traum* (Ger. dream).
Do you know
the derivation of the term?
Why not?
I expect a report by noon today.
Do you know
that residents of the 20th century
have a life expectancy of 1000 years?
I have travelled more by far than Marco Polo,
know more facts by far
than Aristotle; can communicate
to far more people than Demosthenes,
and what if Shakespeare had used a word processor?
I expect a report by noon today.
And what is the one thing you would buy
at any price come age 50?"
Time, I answer without thinking,
control over time, so I could freeze it,
store it, unthaw it at will,
color it with the the brightest tinctures,
taste it and at once restore it,
not in me, never once to absorb it inside me.

It is nearly noon, European Summer Time.
In California I'd surely still be dreaming.
At home in EDST there'd be a fighting chance.
Alpentraumer, Alpentraumer,
I may have made up the word, dare I confess it
to someone who's saving African babies
from death before birth?

From the top of the Alps the snow melts.
A white mist, almost Chinese.

6. *Test*

Can you distinguish
the flawlessly painted orchard
outside the window
from the salottino's tapestry of Eden,
its hand-stitched birds, red silk fruit?
Can you distinguish
the village from the tapestry,
the silence from the solace,
the need to dream from the
need to sleep, deeply and without
a single ripped thread, paradise,
a skin so tightly woven
you will not be the least bit tempted
to test the redness of its inner lining?

Now:
Balance the snow and the palmtrees
without disturbing either.

Do not give misty, ambivalent answers.
The locked gates
with the seamless horizon,
the grand salon's black sealed Bechstein
with the birdcries,
the *a capella* wind chorale.

Do not give misty, ambivalent answers.
When will it come,
in what shape?
Will it never come and will
that be enough?

What is the connection, if any,
between the words *trauma* (Gk. wound)
and *traum* (Ger. dream)?

Do not give misty, ambivalent answers.

7. *The Black-Shawled Women*

No Alps at all today.
A fog so thick and unyielding
I could be anywhere.

The black-shawled old women
last week on the bench at Cadenabbia,
nearly toothless, a dialect so obscure
I could only nod and smile.
For all I know
they spoke to me of death, of cheese,
   of *Alpentraumer*.
The two black-shawled women
are stirring huge kettles
on the other side of the fog.
Chopping garlic.
Scraping goat-dung from the stones.

Nonsense. I have no idea
where the women are
yet can say as well
they have no idea
they've been locked inside this poem.
If they ever heard it
they would, I am sure,
nod and smile.

8. *I Begin*

to arrange things, to own.
Mussolini sleeps
dreamless as the Alp across the lake
now that I've reproduced its curves and crags
in my sketchpad.

The quay and ferry slip
that seemed at first to fade
and scatter from my swaying balcony
I've walked into place;

The churchbells' predictable rituals.
Only the foghorns' chance music
cannot be measured or held;
only the shapes of those faces
most distant at this moment
cannot be exiled
to one of the mind's remote islands.

Slowly the familiar faces stream
to this dreamless dream-country,
fade, scatter, invade again
on their own.

9. *What You See, You* . . .

The Chinese emperors swore
the earth was a flat bolt of silk
with grids that matched its warp and woof.
No need to correct the error.
Likewise in ancient Egypt, where the moon
was a goose to guard the global egg.
In Peru the sages decreed
the earth a lidded box
with an attic apartment for the gods.
What *is* it I expect? A dream
so dogmatic, so real,
I can cease to believe

in maps, laws, anything
beyond the inward eye?
Even if it came, the dream, the dream,
Lago di Como, clear and shining
today in the snowlight,
would have to be muddy brown
as the inner linings of my eyelids.

10. *Alpentraumer*

Dogs howl from the sleeping village, wind
demands entry to the room that clings
like tattered skin.

Immaculate villa, elegant tomb,
you hold no secrets after all,
your flowers bloom

with silk and porcelain tongues. 3 a.m.
The hall telephone rings;
nobody bothers to answer. Who would call

the dead? Fingerprint the sealed Bechstein,
break its black heart
so gusts of music fling themselves

inside the dreamless sleep of all
these honored guests? Gothic piffle,
gilded kitsch. I want it on the cheap,

a message so stunning
there would be no need to think.
Alpentraumer, white dreams, a fright

safe and predictable as the slink
and plunge of a roller-coaster. Across
the mountains the black-shawled women blink.

Their inner theatre unreels
a spectacle so perilous with ice and snow
the women plunge

into a hut of sleep
where white-smocked nurses
treat their wounds with salves

drawn from Alpine bark, the burst
pods of wild flowers.
The women sleep on. Of course.

They have dreamt without knowing what
or if they have dreamt.
As I myself might or might not

have lifted the lid from forbidden urns,
forbidden self. *Alpentraumer, Alpentraumer,*
snow, palms, closed, open,
black piano, white mist.

Coda

At last.
A red-haired Russian
opens the Bechstein,
plays ragtime, blues, all the gypsy-Slavic-
vaguely Jewish music
to which I dance my solitary tangos.
Tonight we all sing. The villa guests;
rumpled bureaucrats from Moscow;
sleek bureaucrats from Washington.
And though one might question
the significance of singing
"We Shall Overcome" in such a place,
for once no hidden meanings,
the piano is open,
no need to dream
or even crave
the secret disclosures of dream-speech.

616 171